SMITTEN PALIMPSEST

SMITTEN PALIMPSEST

POEMS

KENT JENSEN

Smitten Palimpsest: Poems
Kent Jensen

Printed in the United States of America

First Printing, 2024

ISBN 979-8-9906518-0-7
Cover/Interior Design: Knail, LLC

To my parents, Richard and Karen,
who gave me a love for words.

TABLE OF CONTENTS

Foreword . . . xi
Preface . . . xiii
Introduction . . . xix

SECTION I

POEMS

I Without . . . 1
Sing the Christ . . . 4
Knock of Your Be . . . 7
Classic Grey Zone . . . 10
Sworn . . . 14
Alway . . . 15
The Unreasoned Infinite . . . 16
Midsee . . . 18
Downset . . . 21
They Abound . . . 22
Wondrous Opulence . . . 24

None . . . 30
Gain . . . 32
At Times I . . . 34
My Place . . . 35
Atempo . . . 36
Thews . . . 37
Van Allen Belt . . . 38
To Dare . . . 45
fl oz . . . 48
For Perch And . . . 54
Our Middle Grand . . . 56
Stavery . . . 64
You Sap . . . 69
Few Line Suite . . . 80

SECTION II

Addendum: Early Sundry . . . 85

POEMS

[untitled] . . . 89
Bold . . . 90
To Praise You . . . 92
Reign . . . 93
Union . . . 94
Sweet Rain . . . 100

Sans Égal 102
New Words 103
Jesus Dear Friend 104
Electric Majestic Light 105
As I Am 106
Pining 108
Aeroplay 109
Voice and Frame 110
Holy Days 112
Source 115
Pour 116
There Did There Walk 117

WORD OF THE DAY

remeHebegin 120

FOREWORD

He once designed a book for me,
And now he's writing poetry.
—Phil Vischer

PREFACE

Algy met a bear,
The bear was bulgy,
The bulge was Algy.

—Anonymous[1]

Growing up my parents kept a book of poetry on a shelf in the living room. With its faded blue fabric wrap, dogeared corners, and near 600-page bulk it had presence. But more compelling were the poems it contained, which engaged me as I read and re-read them. Those lines introduced me to greater- and lesser-known poets, rhythm and rhyme, structured poetry, and free verse. They intrigued me, offering fun and new discovery with each reading.

The poem above (penned by the both very famous *and* lesser-known poet, Anonymous) was one of my favorites. It still makes me smile, this brief tale of poor

1 Helen Ferris, ed., *Favorite Poems Old and New* (New York: Doubleday & Company, Inc., 1957), 361.

Algy. At a glance it's simply entertaining, granted at Algy's expense. It also holds a moral: steer clear of hungry bears. Yet now, with some years and experience, I see there's more to it. I appreciate the economy of words, the meter and flow, the witty conclusion. With its beginning, middle, and end this poem is complete—a tidy package, simple and simply crafted with care. A gift. To me it achieves the standard spoken of by poet Samuel Taylor Coleridge, "Poetry: the best words in the best order."[2]

I wouldn't say this is the only poem or the only style of poetry I'm drawn to. It is merely an early favorite, an example used here to illustrate that poetry at its finest *resonates* on some level. And it resonates often because it *reveals*: gems, a new perspective, truth. Though sometimes hidden, these things are a birthright for us all. They are worth pursuing.

It's been said, "The job of the poet ... consists of placing those objects of the visible world which have become invisible due to the glue of habit, in an unusual position which strikes the soul and gives them a tragic force."[3] And similarly,

2 Samuel Taylor Coleridge. AZQuotes.com, Wind and Fly LTD, 2024. https://www.azquotes.com/quote/60754, accessed February 12, 2024.

3 Jean Cocteau. AZQuotes.com, Wind and Fly LTD, 2024. https://www.azquotes.com/quote/1224303, accessed February 12, 2024.

"Poetry lifts the veil from the hidden beauty of the world, and makes familiar objects be as if they were not familiar."[4] In this, poetry provides a valuable service.

Since the Fall creation has lost its original luster.[5] Wonders previously visible have become not visible, veiled. Life can be beautiful, yes, but it isn't the perfect garden it once was. Of course the lives we live and the world we live in are worthy of our attention regardless. They do indeed contain deeply moving, amazing aspects. But our ability to discern those is often dimmed by lack of interest, over-familiarity, and our own fallen nature—our inability to see. We simply don't have unobstructed glory-eyes. That aside, we should strive to be actively curious, to be engaged in the pursuit and appreciation of life.

Poetry is not the only means of uncovering deep truths. Nor does every poem contain hidden wonders. Poetry is, however, a device through which new insight can be gained. Through poetry it is possible to see the world around us more completely, with a fresh perspective. And in so doing, we may catch a glimpse of God.

4 Percy Bysshe Shelley. AZQuotes.com, Wind and Fly LTD, 2024. https://www.azquotes.com/quote/269611, accessed February 12, 2024.

5 Romans 8:20–21

God is the perfect poet.

—Robert Browning, poet[6]

God, as our Creator[7], stamped all things with His trademark. Among others, poet Gerard Manley Hopkins[8] considered God and His creation a worthy topic to showcase in verse. He wrote, "All things therefore are charged with love, are charged with God and if we know how to touch them give off sparks and take fire, yield drops and flow, ring and tell of him."[9] Hopkins did indeed know how to wield fire in his poetry and to—with great effect—tell of Him.

Since becoming a Christian in college I've sought to do the same. At first it was through painting, and since then graphic design. Throughout I've also written worship songs. And increasingly of late, poems—some of which have themselves become songs. My hope with these is to offer fresh insight that may spark something in you, that may point you to God.

I've read enough poetry reviews to know some poetry is considered accessible, and some

6 Robert Browning. AZQuotes.com, Wind and Fly LTD, 2024. https://www.azquotes.com/quote/38913, accessed February 12, 2024.

7 Genesis 1:1, John 1:3

8 If you haven't yet, check this guy out.

9 Humphrey House, ed., *The Note-Books and Papers of Gerard Manley Hopkins* (London and New York: Oxford University Press, 1937), 342.

less so—the latter requiring more of its reader. Mine is perhaps a mix. I started out with straightforward verse (see "Reign" and other Section II poems) and have since developed a new palate (see the more recent "You Sap"—an epic celebration of the myriad uses for tree sap.)

In my progression as a poet, I've made use of traditional forms, free verse, rhyming and non-rhyming line endings—all standard devices. I've crafted complex inner structures such as in "Sing the Christ" where the beginning sound of the last syllable in certain lines dictates the beginning sound of the first syllable of the next line (see "be" and "Bold", lines 1 and 2, et al.) I've created new words and phrases as needed: "againing," "flowly," and "scarce well-nigh" to name a few. I've folded foreign language into the mix, explored the lyrical and non-lyrical, and at times—for effect—used imperfect grammar.

Again, these devices are nothing new in the world of poetry. I liken it to exploration in the visual arts—artistic cobbling, with its deconstruction and (sometimes) reconstruction. It's dressing an existing message in new clothes for the sake of creating a unique look. And with that, perhaps a deeper understanding of what's there.

The end result may require more of you, the reader. You may not quite follow some of it the first time through. (I, for one, know *exactly* what I'm saying in these poems.) If that's the case, simply enjoy the word soup. One can find value and beauty in a good mess—take some abstract art, for example—even it if doesn't completely make sense.

That said, I have crafted these for connection. Do take a second look. Read on. You may be surprised at what you find.

INTRODUCTION

> **pal·imp·sest** (păl'ĭmp-sĕst')
> n. Material, as vellum, that is used
> after having been written upon before
> and often shows traces of imperfectly
> erased writing.[10]

A list of tools of the trade for writers is likely to include a keyboard, monitor, possibly a phone note taking app. In past decades this list included a typewriter and paper. And for some—this century or last—an inviting swivel chair, solid oak desk, and vintage wire basket to one side.

A writer needs such things to grow seeds of inspiration; to take early notes through tended middle round drafts to the final written harvest. Along the way, unused ideas fall to the side. The

10 *Webster's II New Riverside Dictionary* (New York: Berkley Books, 1987), 506.

wire basket—vintage or virtual—fills with scrapped efforts.

My tools for the initial writing phase are a notebook, pencil sharpener, and pencil. The eraser end of the pencil is capped with yet another; one eraser not being enough.

A lot of jotting happens—adding, removing, revising, surprising. Irregular rolled eraser peels collect on par with pencil lead and wood shavings. Such defines industry. Such is the process.

I've described this, my creative writing process, in the poem "Stavery." Several lines in there's mention of an "enlightened, wisened, smitten palimpsest." At the very least, the palimpsest part of that phrase is bound to happen; smudged notebook paper a bit worked over, over and again used. In the end, it will wear a finished poem. And it will sit, this paper under that poem, better than it started, even with—no, *because of*—the smudges.

I could elaborate here on how we humans might be compared. How we at times are like that paper: worked over, pared down, uplifted—improved. *Smote* as it were, for good use by a good and loving

Someone. I could elaborate, but I won't. Maybe another time.

So, as stated, achieving palimpsest status is a near-guarantee for paper in my process.

Can the paper additionally be called enlightened and wisened?

One can hope.

And if it then becomes smitten—a variant of smite: to impress powerfully, to affect[11]—I can say in the writing, yes it does.

Whether equal impact carries through *in the reading* is only for you to say.

One can hope.

11 *Webster's II New Riverside Dictionary* (New York: Berkley Books, 1987), 652.

SECTION I

I Without

Swath me
Mendicant
Phylum: Dependent
Ceremonially
Christen me
Lacking
Me scant
Me needy

Picot hands out
Edging
Encircling (had
I more)
Framing

Wholly had I more
Whew—yet mere
Scintilla still
Schlock really
This more-smock
Thin frangible
Gaberdine
Seeded weave

Drear warp and woof
Of death
Wax-coated weft
Cerecloth

Shear such
Shed
Disrobe of this
So-called
Much

I have
I bring
Not
I Without

Nevertheless
These
Factor these

A territory
Determined
By the grace
Of some Another
Has
That one Other

A breath held
Awaited
For need-state
Abated
Has breath

A lost and deficient
Hoping that
Nouveau riche moment
Has hope

Factor these

Breath
And grace
From one Other
In Whom I hope

I without
Am not without

Sing the Christ

Glory be
Bold promise made
Mild manger-answer
So laid

Child adorned
Deep eventide
Tend low dun amblers
Beside

Decked aglow
Gild tidings rain
Right angels ample
Proclaim

Showers spark
Said skies alight
Laud crystal anthems
This night

Herald-brought
Bowed giftings rare
Ring honor wise of
Afar

Parcel rough
Wrought shepherds same
Seek lifting voice to
The Name

Seeing new
No better scene
Sets husbandman still
Serene

Faith at length
Long-pondered deep
Dear Mary's Hope held
Here sleeps

Pre-thorn smooth
Sent swaddled skin
Sweet Babe the Balm of
Our sin

Son in flesh
From Father thus
The Christ Immanuel
With us

Spirit trill
The Godhead sing
Sound Triune songram
Gifting

Laud the earth
In worship gaze
Glad generations
Shall praise

Sing Noel
New radiant tines
The Gift resplendent
Divine

Sing the Christ
Come faithful voice
Vibrance sonorous
Rejoice!

Knock of Your Be

Hard line balk
friend
Made most
'Pon knock

Drawn on into
Yea onto
Away

Stave most
Strayed
Staid
Pending

A tricky
Heart this
Unseen
friend
Knocking just

For
What—
My me?
Pity's sake?

Knocking when
What—
Life clocking?
Reserves
Using?

Knocking so
What—
Boldly?
Unduly?

Knocking at
What—
All?

Too forward this
Made most
His
Hand sans

Without
What—
Worth?

To laugh!
Said some
Ha!
Oh sad mirth
Come!
Know the worth!
Know the worth!

Sad
Too sad
Tragic sad
To miss
Like this
Life

Try
Do try
Said some
Do answer
The most important knock of your be
And see
Like we
Friend

Classic Grey Zone

PART I

Classic
Grey zone
Albeit known
Much much
So say they
For grey

Massive
Untouched side
Obtuse
Fierce
Angle slide
For obscure

Hide stock
Fiercely
Backside

I'd
Such such
Seen
Felt keen
Same grey
Came stayed

Cloud
Alongside
For
Days for

Hiding
As it were
Unobserving
Obscured stock
Grey mock

Faux lock this
Blocking
Shading yes
Thus
Poser though
Knowing poser

All weak
All large show
Smoke
Mere smoke

PART III

Seasoned winds
Blow flavor
Bland mess
This
Dull
Dead
In need
Disperse

PART IV

What hidest
Though shroud?

Only that
Allowed

Subject

Coarse
Quick passing
This
To posing
Transparent

Token nod
To subjected empty
To
That which
Masks-ish
God

Sworn

Rough hewn
Quick cut
Lecherous rogue
Lumber rot

Semi restrain-ed
Roustabout naught
Aught-worker hack

Prickly slivered rack
Fracas
Et barreling non
So so
Sworn

Amongst preening
Libertine
Leaning
Curse-ed pace-ed rove

Alway

The Lord
With great
Attentive
Love rent blood
Attuned
Not newly
Knowing
Alway

The Unreasoned Infinite

Large
Too small a
Word

Largest close
Yet not
A notch just
Single
Above last

Lacking
Unit even
Step click tic
None
To measure
This One by

Additions regular
Stacked
Succeeding
Do not achieve
To infinitive

Defined
Points joined

Careful mark
Continuous
Does not
Surround Boundless
Cannot

Immeasurable then yet
Closer
Yet beyond yet

Set aside
Convention
Determinates
Webster exhaustive
Delineates
Step outside increments
Relatable
Reason

The Unreasoned Infinite
Is quite
Non-boundary
Non-analogy
Quite
Non-simply
Other than

Midsee

Barren lands
Soul strewn
Between
Paychecks

Pay pay
This pay

Nemesis

Necessary evil
Yes?
Well—needed
Just

Our God owns
This land
Barren
Newing
Abundant
Strewn
Thriving

Look to Him
Soul midwith
Hovering

In a sense
Falling yes?
Forward
Yes
Moving thus

Now
Out aired
Flailing and
Sailing and

Oh
Land that
Plant pregnant
Step
Already

Midstride I
In flux

Stand though
Midsee
Do
Pre-pay
Pre-dirt!
Impossible?
Stand the step
Next
Best planted
Midair
Well before
Terra
Faux firma

Trust

Downset

Let a one
As such
Said pilgrim
Sunk
Sing linger lines
Along a lane
Song long
Selah

Drawn
Dour days
Downset
Kismet praise
Translucent dawn

Drink
Said soul
Praise dregs
Downed
Pilgrim drunk
Once sunk
Soar

Said soul
Arise

They Abound

"And now, dear believing reader, rejoice and praise with me."

—George Mueller

"What shall I render to the LORD?"

—Psalm 116:12

They abound
Dear reader
Reasons
Yea profound
Fundamental
Seek worthy
Central
And plain

I implore
In light
Claim cite
The multitudes

As once
Inquired 'What
Shall I render
To the LORD?'
Acknowledge

And rejoice
Swoon
Sing the grand
Holy profferings

Come let
Gratitude
I implore let
Lavish
Approval imbue
Your inmost being
Corm-deep
Infusings
By which by
Nature
Nourish and grow
The whole
Into one
Worshipful
Thankful
Joyous

Wondrous Opulence

PART I

Ebbing blue
Swirls a tincture true
Skies a-roam
High seas ho!
Brine and foam

Geo depth
Heft defining heft
Strata grey
Underlay
Stoic staid

Yet said rift
Holding patterns shift
Lilt and spin
Swimming skin
Fire therein

Churning green
Base and breath unseen
Moss on stone
Grass and loam
Leaf-life blown

Gold of God
Seeded over sod
Offers ore
Breath absorbs
Covers orb

In the skies
Seas unvaporize
Recontain
Housing rain
Douse again

Thunderbolt
Particles in molt
Dark charge rends
Lean light lends
Palate cleansed

Swirling light
Not quite seen to sight
Rays ray clear
Paints appear
There and here

Colors yon
Vivid spectrum spawn
Lush by law
Also awe
Seeing saw

Hearing hear
In electric ear
Sparkle pound
Blare flares sound
Roaring 'round

Hushes mur
Breezes soft concur
Slight to small
Audible
In one's soul

Still small voice
Spoken overjoys
Senses when
Wo and men
Hear again

Maker's pip
Makes one's spirit skip
Rouse from sleep
Quicken, keep
Deep to deep

PART II

Call to me in myriad varied hues
Call me languid not
Call true

True me out and glory in Your splendor
  in the round
Abound One wild and wondrous Form
Shine sweet particulate soundings on
Yea anon

One speck astounding
Next to nothing floors
One pip
Shoring glory viz quip
Goldentine adorning Maker's lip

True

Bespoke the formless form
From void to shade
From floor to wade
Foundations laid
Breathmomentmade
Delight cascade
Made languid not

Call wondrous opulence

PART III

Wonders score
Tens—nay *millions*—more
Master-planned
Plated and
From His hand

Overlap
Plaided systems strap
All to one
Spinning spun
Amalgam

Woven wrought
Spoken languid not
For these three:
You and me
His glory

None

Greater
Love was love
None

Wondrous such
Spoken
For before I

Prepared
Given
Detail spared
None

Savior's life
Disdained
My
For me
Laid claim
Very blood
For
Me in love
And shame

You came
Intent
In victory
Given

For me
Death
Slain

Sweet sacrifice
Of heaven

Gain

Shaken core
Gain resolve
Parched and weak
Begin

Selah stir
Treasure trove
Seeker read
Begin

Spirit soar
Soothing salve
Cover me
Begin

Let a heart
Filled with love
So now speak
Begin

Laud th'more
Quench and crave
deep to Deep
Begin

Hearer hear
Saviorlove
Come and have
Sin-wagemeet
Heaven seat
Life replete

Begin

At Times I

Whisper
'I love you' Lord
By God
By good
You
Have I do know
Graces
You have shown
As always
Grace is
Here was be
Ever oh
Will

Be ever
Oh this I've
Known yet
In my
Soul at
Times I
In part
Sway feign heart

My Place

For God
This song
Set far
This long
Heart unset
Far too long

Here
Tend release
Forthwith
My me
Placed

God
For He saves for
Song

Can
For so loved so
Forthwith
Placed

So tend release

Atempo

Word of Life
Each saving pulse

Beating out
A tempo thus

Word then Life then Word then Life

Thews

Amen
So stand
My
Way I'm
Again set
Amend met

Van Allen Belt

In
May surmise
There one
With skies
Two

Deux
(So deduced)
Quay-like
(Dos pseudos
though) zones
Milky
Way-like (*fakes!*)
Wharfs
Sans stanchions
Abrupt
Broad walk
Bind banks
Stellar

Where
Stations there
Unloaded

New lauds
Prayers and
To God plash
Barely can
Soft land en masse
Magno-
Electrically drawn
To a halt
A la
Van Allen belt

Inept (they infer
Wrongly)
Sent kept
Wearied dimmed
Cinched
Steeped
Static and stepped
Straps two
Dampening
Pair strongly per
(So say)
So trapped
Ne'er to pass

Levels these
Thee girthing
Giving Earth
Wing-ed breezed
Those
From souls set sail
In thin hopes
Little faithlets
Flown
Unsure-ing
God hearing
Instead
Upcaught flotsam fearing
Broken donedrifts
Sounding not
Heard not

Inert
Not sown
Neo-dormant
Insignificants
Extracted ore
Spent
And lo untended
Electric life-charge
Darkened drained

Unflushed
Leaf piles blown
Aloft
Soft-crushed
Deadened
So ended

Thus
Soul dutiful
Assumes
Ode beautiful
Stale
Pale notions

Rote writ
Wrought
For naught
Soul recite
Slight
Repeat

Life cries
Guessed lifeless
Land
'Pon ceiling bands
Depleted

Such the whim
Of the
Unrepleted

Yet listen Nations
Realmente not so
That's not
How it like
Works yo
God hears
Actualmente and
How always
And
Verdaderamente even
Now

Wavering none
Of sent rent waves
No heaven-short
Cast no
Petering-prone
No heart cry missed
Yes
Nary a one

Know Nations this
God hear is
For Him
To Him
By Him
Through Him

And so on go
Moreover seek
Exercise
Foundational
Interlanguage role
Reap
Beyond on
Seeker on
This core
Arrangement
Our deep to Deep
Call-response
Engagement

Voice!
Then Nations
Use words
Use heart
Chase and pray

So reply
For ours
Reach believe
People ours
Is to respond
God is *in call*
Has called
Into life each
Engage therefore enthuse
Send praise rage
Muse

All to Him
Enter in
Proclaim
Sustain and soar
Incline
So shine
God-intertwine
All th'more

To Dare

I lope up
And down
Step unseen-ic
Ground

Some my grain
Divide
In a ripsaw
Stride

Rivet raw
Core sing
Carpe diem
Ing

Would that all
Were same
Save for lesson
Gain

On road alt
Cut cross
Seamy tempest
Tossed

Fenceless posts
Slip past
Pitching flailing
Fast

Sprawling waste
Lame land
Best to quick cleave
And

Note the mark
Felt score
Visit never-
More

Sever loss
Begot
Heed it little
Thought

Garner fresh
Resolve
Treasure measured
Rove

For ahead
The prize
Venture press on
Thrive

fl oz

Pick
Of anything
A peck
Step
With tape
An acre trod
Take
Breath drawn
Measured
Invisible
Volume on

Survey
That gaseous
Appraise
Liquid states
All solids
Careful now
Approach
Confident
With engaged
Now-thoughtfulness
See

Adamantly day
The micrometer
Best in hand
To attend

Light the tray
Inquisitively pan
Miniscule
To enormous
Invite
Haul
Ask ask

Hoist
That device rod
Mark
Move
Repeat

Sterile dish
A-ready
Beseeming befit
Furnishable and
Supply
Wisely
Blithely

Appreciate
The dawn
Ingots of know
Hitherto
Sowed
And reaped
In the cleaving
Of summed up
Defining

Celebrate
That dawning that
Way new
Named
Once that
Some old day
When one
Shall we call *Definder?*
When one
Definder
Uptaking
God's bounty
Lofting
Saw

Newly viewing
Sought for
Proclaiming

On quintal!
I shall bushel!
We achieve
Dram assign
Hectare!
One scruple one
Barrel please
If I may
Many grains weigh
The ton
Long short metric
Ahoy!
Nautical and
Otherwise miles
Leagues
Seek on
Parsec
Parse the minim
I dub thee
Cubit
And pace that span

Behold it
Squared
Encase and hold
It cubed
A la stere
Furlongs and stadia
Shall coexist
Compliment
Pour aplenty
Litres homers pints
So received
Wet or dry

Be pleasantly fixed
You standards
Scales and units
Kept
For to collect

Observe these
Oh Countrymen
Ever at
Inclined
Useful beings
There disposed

For our
On the explore
Gladly assist
Our own
Fresh findings and
Deft
Uptakings of
This
God's great
Bounty

For Perch And

Crow's nest
Of sorts those
For
Perch and
Bob awhile

One can guess
Tiny heart
Smiling rest
Breathing
Be

Taking whole
Digest
All cool degrees
Visible round
In-nostril
Ingest
View-breaths
Tasting

Weighting
Cool breeze
Adjust

Light lurch
Slighting
Lob
Ever so

Stop and chirp
Perchgaze
Appreciate
Segue sing
Gale again

Our Middle Grand

PART I

Eyes long
On sky span
Horizon

Grand where
Here
Burning blue
Informs tan
Ocean-
And sand-
Like
Here
The range
Noncoastal
The ground
Expanse
Our
Middle grand

Like the
Edges
This ground has

A grain
A wave
To it

Like the
Our outline
Blue is
Titan
Great in
Depth in
Its highing
Outerlying

PART II

Swirl
Evening
Middle ground sky
Gradate great
Heights
Pink
Cerulean blue
Toward night
Watercoloring
To dark
Rich

Dusted lit
Tips of tines
Upon climb
Peek
Skip
Keep
Pattern
Lattice
Slowly
Circulating

Deep
Constellations
Consider
Dinner plate
White
Up over
Singular bright
Hover
Illuminated
Still life

Slow
Now-sun
Unstilling
Softly

Earthroam
Forthwith
Daybending
Deftly
Leaning
Into waking
Songbrewing
Now-drone
Into aroma
Color
Bright crystalline
Soundings

Swarm skin
Chime
Earthenly
Sing
Buffalo tones
Grass runes

Anteloping
Tendrils combing
Post prairie
Schooner
Off paths
Free
From obstructions

Wander
Swift fox
High plains
Bison graze
God-irrigated
Tallgrass
Amongst
Nonparallel
Corrugates
Teeming
Pocket mouse
Et al
All one
Biome

PART IV

Windbreeze
Currenting
Eddy pools
Rise skyside
Blend
Carry pure
Dayclear
To first
People's
People
Continue

Air
Fair conduit
Invisible
Sides
Horizon wide
Keen
Loyal housing
Hot harsh
Variations
Humid
Cold
In steady
Rotating

Blue white
Supply

Faintly
Beginning
Twilight tine tips
Blink forth
Againing

PART V

Still warm
Hence
Strata
Fragrantly
Exhales
Interior
Trade winds
Shoal
The ecozone
Refrains
Hums
Happily trailing
Then sleepily
Off as
Is the tend

Daily commence
Permeate
Shading
Sated privileged
Inner land

Stavery

Word mead
Poured page
Gain rivulet
Burgeon
Rage

Culled
Heartfelt
Parlance upon
Rich sage
Vellum
To wit
This (and
Others)
Scrivener stream
Courses
Enlightened
Wisened
Smitten
Palimpsest

To achieve
Assayer
Gauges

The keeps (the
Gems) the
Eraser-thems
Such passed
Scribblings-ash
Sent
Brushed parings
A-wind went
In lieu
Yea into
The Minto Basin
Scrapped
For favored
Scored over
Savory
Afters

Select
Connected
Cursive concepts
Left
Distilled
Heard-abouts
Mutual
Taken-part-ins
Never-knews now

Treasured inklings
Newly
For to appreciate
With contemplate

Purveyed
Compellings
Aloft alight
Curated Specials
Plated
Insight
For to absorb

Our writ
Denominator
The human
Experience
Via choice
Chosen
Morsels

Dearest vim
Considered
Vigor artistry
Figured
These deemed

And held
In high regard

Wrote
Speech sounds
Seeking
Wonder
Souls smote
Voltage captured
Raw
Wrought
Maximus

Trace
Beauty messed
Revealed
Each
Graffito steeped
Zested
To taste
These
Distinct
Decidedly
Abiding
With kinsmen
United

Goal golden
Succulent
Scrumption
For to
Consumption
Lo
Inspiration
Revelation

Go!
Flume-flown élan
Ho!
Fly alive line
Life-supply
Set
Glistening
Oeuvre rivulet!
And to nourish
Roam
Con brio
Stand
To ring true and
Ride
Rio Grande wide

You Sap

You sap

Stop!
Not *this* a dupe
No roped slow
Such nope
Crude knot ooze
Much more so
Is so
There-
Fore exudes hence
I commence
The pitch

Be introduced
Herein
To resin
And through-states
Most alternate

Industrious
Phloem et flow
Git goo
From the go

In-tar be to
Considered curious
Untempered potential
As realized is
Richness
In viscous

Initially guessed
Worthless?
Hot mess?
Noil use? There
Uncrucially?
Spare?
Au contraire

Honey from a tree
They learn-ed
Piqued
Then where when
What and how
Do we?

Entails proceed
Parlay
Fail pry

Known needs be-try
Be fixed
Possibilities seen
Barriers
To discovery blown
Upon uncovery
Tacky contributionist
Enhancement
Bridge
Betwixt

Promoted
Woody body blood
Day job
Duty did
Paladin
Does
Feeded tree seed
And yon
Goes out
The glistening morn
Askance none
From vital
Home fires kindler
So set tending yet
On-ending

Hammertoe bends
And truer limbs

Yes out onward
Assuming
In elevated ask
Unbound post-house
Heave-to-airy
Ventures

Oakum-like
Nichen found
Arken
Quite said
Not the least
Stickywood
Wickiups
Sticks and boats all
Canvas
Like-tied go
Tidied wa-
Tertight sided
Saw so
Set to sail
Landward ho

Plies
Pithwith slip
Nutty
Nongrain balm
Onto panned
Bars and cakes
Con regularity that
Ikon syrup
(So pines molasses)
Amberclear fix
Of yokel hick
And early Mountie
Aplenty
Y the masses
And

Y knack status
Drop
Topical anesthetic
Tap
Sealant pat healant
Take
Two chew for
Sore throat
Sick
Ingredient

Slick chicle
Sip
Rip tea
Lick tea

Viscid sublimate
Drained
In writ wrapped strips
Morphs acceptance
Socially
Astraining from
Normative mode
To new abodes
High sea lows
Exploratory
Beckon wide
Advancing halls
Lab-
Oratory-grab
The new next gain
Thunder unmain
Engine roads
Met soundly
At that compelling
Perigee
Accel'ing roundly

Walled
Squash confines
Et al
Quash pleasant
Staccato
Impact echoes
Reveal
Heartily mealings of
Glowing
Healthen practice
Numerative
Aids made mobile
You see
By our
So our friend
Defines
To fund
Go-methodology
Globally

Antique
Resinite seams
Baltic
Shine this
Petrographic
Resonator

Ambrite seems
Unphased
Upon meeting brighten
New Zealand air
Anew
Twain ex
Again seemingly
Unpetrified
Yeah no
(Though actually
So)
Old-timey
Sent sunward
Gibraltar
Undone excels
Speaks
Twain ex et
Once alone
A polish given
Shone
Aligns nicely
Near ear collar bone
And secondary amix
Scent one-ward
Met by first
Inclusion-free

Gem set
Both un-visibly
And visibly
Elavishly
Emit

Without sound
Wound and gut
Strings found
Horse hairs slide
Not saying
Aside
Not playing
Glide not befit
Beside it
Woe
Unlit
Racked rows bowed
Sans lack
However
Shower rippling bands
Mellow waves
Reverb again
Cello burn
So the torch
Same

In none
Meh
Plain
But tend
So to mend
Oh stave flame

Righteous
Deciduous fuel
You'll say
Say pin-ay-
See-eye
Bon conifer knows
The
(Pin-ay-see-eye)
Slowly flowly
Petrol of the
Cone-bearing
Pinaceae
And smiles

Tall diverse team
Meek
And wild
Diversely
Contributing

Their neo
Non-nettle
Hayseed of sorts
And such
Of great imports
Here near
And there
Hear
The livelong day

Few Line Suite

OX

This times
Cipher sign
Bovinely
Hug with kiss
Which one is?

Perhaps allnly
A few line

XO

What wrought?
Ten I emotes
Aka n n
Sci oxygen
Unknown of note
Equals aught

o

Equals aught
Ness
By its lonesome
Es

x

Holds
Inner and
Out together and
Song none better see
Laminin
In
See knoll
See save fulcrum
See sung toll from

SECTION II

ADDENDUM: EARLY SUNDRY

Early sundry. Previous miscellaneous. Older stuff.

The following pages showcase a selection of poems I wrote before those preceding. I include them to give you a glimpse into my early process via these entry poems. In every way they informed and shaped my current approach to poetry.

You'll note some differences, not the least of which is there are more words per line. Few poems here contain lines with one word. Many poems on previous pages consist almost *entirely* of one- and two-word lines.

There is a more consistent use of rhyming line endings here. The words are less abstract, more conversational, more accessible. I was very much about exploring internal structures (see the repeating internal rhymes in “Aeroplay” and “Voice and Frame”) among other devices and forms.

There is even an old-school iambic pentameter[12] sample (see "There Did There Walk".) The iambic pentameter—known as "the most common meter in English poetry"—was used by greats like Chaucer and Shakespeare.[13]

This is no attempt to place myself in such company. I was merely exploring established forms, seeking to create new ones, and finding my own way to present verse.

I was, and still am, refining a craft.

I do think I've landed on my own "seasoned" approach in the previous set. I plan on continuing in that vein. But there's still some merit in the early attempts, a sampling of which follows.

12 A rhythm designation in poetry which involves "iambs." An iamb is a type of "foot" (or syllable group) with one unstressed and one stressed syllable: da-dum'. An iambic pentameter therefore has five (penta) iambs: da-dum' da-dum' da-dum' da-dum' da-dum'
"Iambic pentameter," Wikipedia, accessed March 2, 2024, https://en.wikipedia.org/wiki/Iambic_pentameter.

13 Ibid.

[untitled]

The sweetness in Your look
The depth of steps You took
Your glory *magnifique*
Enthralls and thrills and floors me
Oh One that I'm adoring
With praises countless pouring

Bold

For us
The raiment of the cross
For once
The heinous taken loss
For all
Would all partake the gold
The gift
The pain and smear of old
The searing sacrifice of depth untold

For all
In this, His gift
His all

All—all!
Sing—sing!
Scarce well-nigh, friends—*sing!*
For all the bounty and the glory and
  the victory He brings
For lo!
Hung bell of death rings life—
Behold!

The cross
For us

Love rung bold!

To Praise You

God Father glorious
In wondrous ways amazing us
Adoring pouring forth
We come
We come to praise You

Christ Savior Majesty
So blazing reigning gloriously
Delighting pining strides
We come
We come to praise You

Ghost Holy powerful
Sweet Godwithus ethereal
Communing swooning runes
We come
We come to praise You

Reign

Father rain down
Measure my soul
Show where I lack
Fashion me whole

Jesus rain strong
Fashion me true
Beautiful rain
Bathe me in You

Spirit rain on
Bathe me profound
Bounty for lack
Passion unbound

Union

The body gathers
True believers
Spirits bent
A building ache

Hearts intent
A body focused
True believers
Truth partake

Take on Body
His sorrowful Passion
Slake this world
The thought thereof

True remembrance
His sorrowful Passion
Take His Body
Take His Blood

Pilgrim pause
With Jesus-focus
Join the stay
The closing throng

Closing in with
Hearts wide open
Hearts intently
Leaning on

Lend intently
Learn in silence
Lean your soul
Come seek be still

Spend it focused
Pause remember
Jesus rent
On Calv'ry Hill

There the Savior
Legion taming
Rights restraining
Holding fast

Staid intent
Intensely reigning
Gaining
Earth about aghast

In the round
Creation rumbled

Stage the epic
Master-strike

Sky to ground
Engaged entumbled
Grey great groaning
Moaning shook

Shifting seismic
Rend sound structure
Boundaries curtic
Tearing shorn

Said division
So divided
God for man through
Crown of thorns

Passion-driven
Lifeway given
Pouring forth
Divine intent

Slain and broken
Blood bespoken
Love adorned as
Sacrament

Gorge this act
Of Christ eternal
Pre-primeval
Origins

Forging back
Beyond primordial
Spanning forth
To cover sins

In the rend
Ne'erending gaining
Soul-deep washing
Sin's death-stain

Gift from Glory
Save-blood given
Free-us reason
For us slain

Godhead bent
Our God in glory
Christ with sorrow
There forsook

Spirit-rending
To the marrow

Triune Godhead
All partook

Carved the cut
The sage Trade Woodsman
Sin-angst ridden
Not His own

Cut the Man
For all His kinsmen
Never greater
Loving shown

Such the Godman
Deep communion
Deeply slaying
Being slain

Grasp the volume
Grasp the length
To which He went
For us to gain

Crown of cause
His sorrowful Passion
Grasp the depth
The width the height

Grasp the breadth
Of Savior suff'ring
Grasp His anguish
In our plight

Take Believer
Here in stillness
Spirit-trek
To DeathLife knoll

Set here honor
Measure Savior
Test His suff'ring
Taste His toll

Test now Blessed
In this moment
Fathom question
Christ, for whom?

Bask in reverence
Taste forgiveness
Hear in stillness
All for you

Sweet Rain

Sweet Rain come wash my being
My sin in desperate needing
Of Your flood
Your given blood

Mud-coated streaked and tainted
My soul a picture painted
Hence my part
To cleanse my heart

Tart alabaster tears
The weeping sting of years
Solemn flow
How to let go

No now or ever after
No past-poured alabaster
Efforts cleanse
My many sins

Sans Christ and His redeeming
Sweet rain-flow wooing streaming
To partake
To soothe and slake

Make null the sin would pin me
Make full the void within me
In You I
Leave death for Life

Strife now though part of living
Fresh hope this Shower giving
Far and nigh
And by and by

I see I'm death without it
With no two ways about it
I submerge
Sweet Holy purge

Sans Égal

The blood of Christ
Brings more to me each day
Each blessed day
Sweet blessings in the washings in the
cleansings of my path

The Bread of Life
Lays soil beneath my roots
Soul-thirsty roots
Base fuel absorbing wholly meeting
fully soul-deep needs

The Name divine
Sheds life within dead void
Dead fetid void
Sends scattering retreating tail-betweening
death to done

The love of Christ
Is sunlight *sans égal*
Beyond compare
Is hope-brimmed golden shimmer rays
that warm past sin's wan scope

New Words

Anew I call
New words I bring
Can't speak to all
You've done for me
My meager most
Not even close
Yet here I try
Anew
Hear
I

Jesus Dear Friend

Jesus dear Friend
Christ my beginning and end
Take what I am

Dye me blood-white
Crimson-cross-washed in my plight
Pure in Your sight

Purchased in pain
Savior in victory slain
Your death my gain

Paid with the thought
I too might give as I ought
My life blood-bought

Have what you see, my Lord

All that I've been and will be
You're my beginning and end
Jesus dear Friend
Take all of me

Electric Majestic Light

Wholly electric around Your throne
Sacred charges for Your own
Wholly magnetic—come now, come all
To know and be fully known

Searing sparkle-ing Savior call
In Your high royal holy hall
Christ Your glory glowing shines
Seeing we before You fall

Radiant Presence be magnified
Jubilant voices sweet given flight
Chorusing praises to You alone
Jesus electric majestic Light

As I Am

Good Lord lone Savior
Could I find favor
And be called Your own
Though in sin as I am?

Might I endeavor
To be close to You?
As close as flaw can be
To Flawless

It makes no sense
This possibility
Of Sinless slain for me
Unless come Calvary
The where it all began
This gift
This chance

Open wide potential

What could come of this?
Might I endeavor
To be close to You?

Could I find favor
And be called Your own
Though in sin as I am?

Sinless says "Yes!
Come into My rest"

Pining

Sovereign Father
Save and Source of Life
Your are my salvation

Sweet Redeemer
Meet me here in my
Deep anticipation

Striving striding
Pining for the One
Singular in grandeur

Of Your equal
Count them there are none
You are like none other

Aeroplay

Overspill
Fast walls foursquare

More than fill
Vast open air

Stars, wonders
Past burning blue

No borders
Cast hold on You

Voice and Frame

You, O Lord
Most glorious above all time
So wonderous in form that I
Boast sonorous in voice and frame

Name, O Lord
Of boast worthy sovereign state
Love showcasing latent strength
Glove potent to hand Divine

Mine, O Lord
'Pon kneeling sinew and soul
On seeing my sin in whole
Yon green pastures offered there

Where, O Lord
Dark Calvary's crooked tree
Mark salvation fields from Thee
Our malfeasance cure if sought

Bought, O Lord
Love spent 'midst a swirling rage
Blood rent in the gift You gave
Come friend taste a wonderous thing

Bring, O Lord
Mass souls to soul-centered end
Past old sins to saving Friend
Vast throes of joy that day seen

Glean, O Lord
Life 'bundantly given free
Strife wondrously struck by Thee
I've numbered my days to come
Highs, lows 'neath the rain or sun
With You, O most glorious One

Holy Days

Lenten span for
Self-imposed halt to relate two score
Slow fast in solemn prayer
Ash Wednesday lead

Rolling excess
Laud fronds ebullient praise en masse
King a-colt amid shouts
Sunday palm rave

New rite take eat
Broken and poured remember repeat
Realized in full day next
Maundy Thursday

Flying above
Agony, redemption rent in love
Christ on the cross in flight
Good Friday wake

Right-siding death
Crest the vivid burning Righteousness
Upsoaring Christ arise
Easter dawning

Translucent shroud
Wonderment gazing Christ into cloud
Assurance Spirit send
Ascension Day

Spiritual sound
In one accord wind tongues all around
Stoking descending Flame
Pentecost might

Gird up heart care
Sole focus set sight to Christ prepare
The coming arrival
Adventen watch

Cold bright firestorm
Night sparkle radiant angels swarm
Crystalline skies a-rush
Twilight Noel

Piercing the din
Manger ray Babe of hope to rescind
Death with visceral Life
Christmas morning

Treasure fourfold
Gifts from the magi and Child foretold
Rejoicing with great joy
Epiphany

Source

If as a tree beside a brook
If as a cloud anew in flight
If as earth yearning thirsting long
I was

I'd find my source to saturate
My drink
My make
My save from drought

In You
Oh Fountain
This my song

Pour

Pure Source of Life
You're more than I
Should store inside

There Did There Walk

There walked
Hear me now
There did there walk a Man

There walked a Man a millionfold to save
A Ransom-Man come in the Father's will
And like the Godhead Rest He pined yet still
He walked in skin
The crux therein

He there did walk a thousand days intent
On giving drop and sinew soul and sleeve
On crushing sting in death and death in life
White-fire-focus stride within the strife
Yet in the Garden asked for a reprieve
He walked in skin
The crux therein

'God let this pass except Thy will be done'
His grieving self asweat with strains of blood
Then in the Garden lo a hundred come
For thirty pieces gain to settle score

The skin befit for angel army care
The crux the crux incarnate lie before
The Ransom-Man of all of this aware
He walked in skin
The crux therein

The twelve accounted come betrayal kiss
His several this mere handful huddled by
So few to watch in prayer nay draw a sword
The sleeping trickle stood all gone awry
His scattered wake then gushed and left the Lord
He walked in skin
The crux therein

A shamble trial before Sanhedrin hence
Preamble to the seething Pilate crowd
Through false besmearing stacked and jeering hate
To save the skin the Christ spoke naught aloud
But rose above His flesh to chosen fate
He walked in skin
The crux

Between two flanked aside displayed and pinned
God-bodied Figure rent deep anguish met
Distraught and pained forsaken still He sought

And gained our ransom skin to crux blood-bought
Achieved His goal to breach the threshold death
For humankind despite that human flesh
He hung in and the agony it meant

Behold the length and breadth and
  depth and height
Of passion cause and suffering combined
A love no greater anyone could find
A love no greater anyone could find
Than One—our Savior—'pon the cross He climbed

WORD OF THE DAY

re•me•He•be•gin (rē′mē-Hē′bē-gĭn)
n. a mnemonic device for sharing the way to new life in Christ. It combines "re: me" (regarding my state) with "He" (God's gift in Christ) and "begin" (my now next step).

---

re: me

for all have sinned and fall short of the glory of God, —Romans 3:23

For the wages of sin is death ... —Romans 6:23a

He

... but the gift of God is eternal life in Christ Jesus our Lord. —Romans 6:23b

For God so loved the world that He gave His only begotten Son, that whoever believes in Him should not perish but have everlasting life. —John 3:16

But God demonstrates His own love toward us, in that while we were still sinners, Christ died for us. —Rev 3:20

Behold, I stand at the door and knock. If anyone hears My voice and opens the door, I will come in to him and dine with him, and he with Me. —Romans 5:8

begin

that if you confess with your mouth the Lord Jesus and believe in your heart that God has raised Him from the dead, you will be saved. For with the heart one believes unto righteousness, and with the mouth confession is made unto salvation. —Romans 10:9–10

Made in the USA
Coppell, TX
14 October 2024

38645534R00085